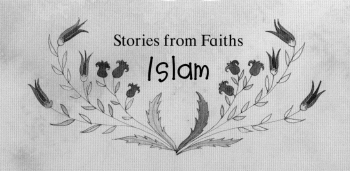

Stories from Faiths
Islam

The Great Night Journey
and Other Stories

First published in the United States by
QEB Publishing, Inc.
23062 La Cadena Drive
Laguna Hills, CA 92653

www.qeb-publishing.com

Library of Congress Control Number: 2007000957

ISBN 978 1 59566 375 7

Written by Anita Ganeri
Design and editorial by East River Partnership
Illustrated by Jenny Reynish
Series Consultant Roger Butler

Publisher Steve Evans
Creative Director Zeta Davies
Senior Editor Hannah Ray

Printed and bound in China

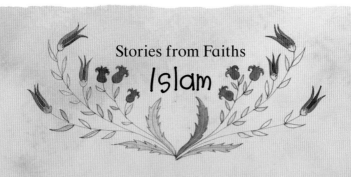

Stories from Faiths
Islam

The Great Night Journey
and Other Stories

Anita Ganeri
Illustrated by Jenny Reynish

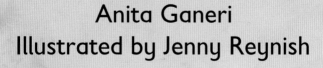

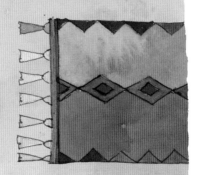

QEB

Muhammad and the Holy Book

Long ago, the Prophet Muhammad lived in the city of Makkah. He married a woman named Khadijah. Muhammad and Khadijah were very happy together.

4

But some people in Makkah were cruel and greedy. They did not treat other people very well. Muhammad did not like the way they behaved.

Muhammad often went to a cave on a
nearby mountain to pray. Sometimes, he
stayed there for many days. He thought
about how to make things better.

One day, an amazing thing happened. A bright light filled the cave, and Muhammad saw an angel. The angel was holding a piece of cloth, which was covered in writing.

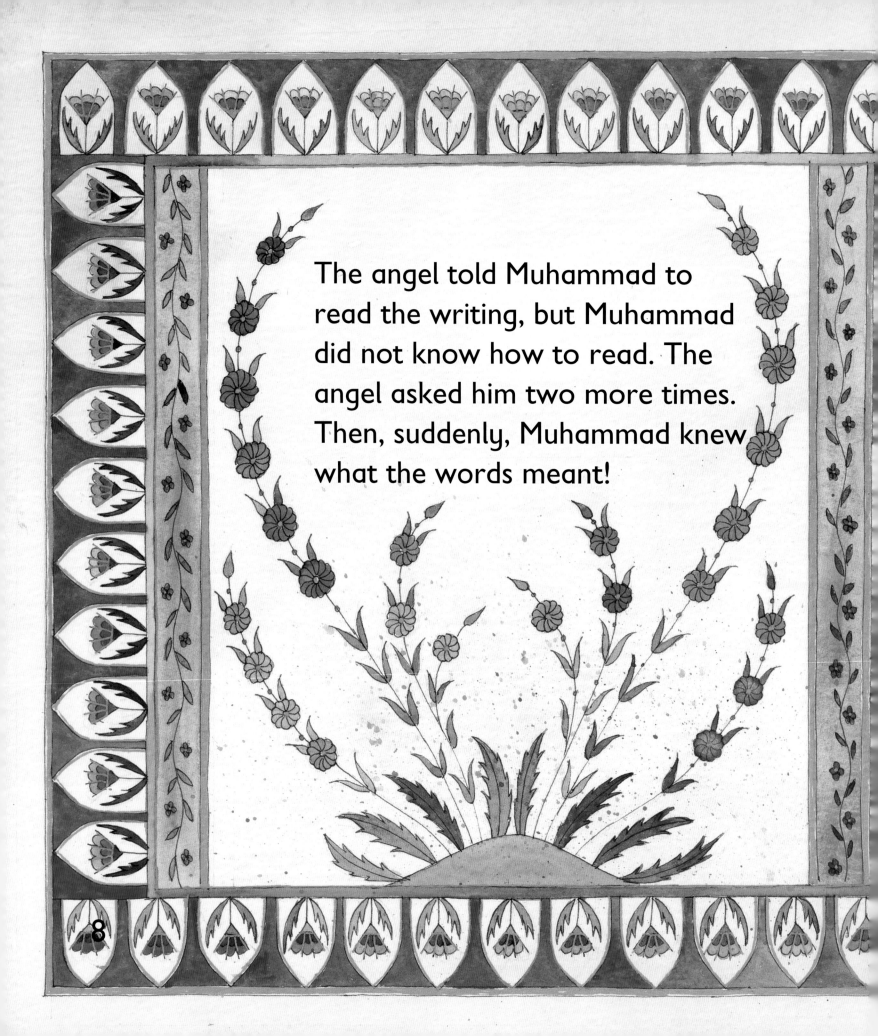

The angel told Muhammad to read the writing, but Muhammad did not know how to read. The angel asked him two more times. Then, suddenly, Muhammad knew what the words meant!

These were Allah's words.
The angel told Muhammad
that Allah had chosen him to
be his messenger. Allah wanted
Muhammad to teach people
how to live a good life.

During his life, Muhammad heard
many more words from Allah.
Sometimes, the angel brought them.
At other times, Muhammad heard a
voice speaking to him. Muhammad
learned all Allah's words by heart.

Muhammad told the words to his friends. Later, his friends wrote down the words in a very special book. It is called the Koran, and contains Allah's words and teachings.

The Great Night Journey

One night, as the Prophet Muhammad slept in his house in Makkah, an angel woke him up. The angel had come to take Muhammad on an amazing journey.

The angel brought a fabulous animal
for Muhammad to ride. It looked like
a snow white horse. Its name was
Al Buraq, which means "lightning."

13

Muhammad, Al Buraq,
and the angel raced
through the skies. When
they reached the city of
Jerusalem, the angel led
Muhammad up into heaven.

In heaven, Muhammad met
the prophets who had come
before him. Like him, they
were Allah's messengers.
They greeted Muhammad
and made him welcome.

15

The angel took Muhammad
into the highest part of heaven.
There, Muhammad was given
Allah's command that Muslims
should say fifty prayers a day.

On his way back down to Earth, Muhammad met the prophet Musa. Musa told Muhammad that fifty was too many prayers for people to say every day.

17

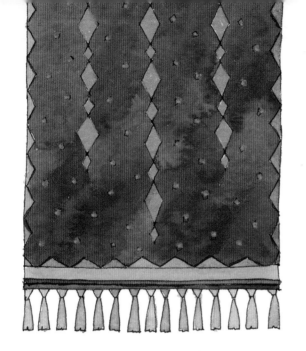

So, Muhammad asked Allah to give him fewer daily prayers. Soon, there were only five prayers left. And that is why Muslims say their prayers five times a day.

The amazing night journey was now almost over. Muhammad climbed onto Al Buraq and flew back to Makkah to tell the people what Allah had said to him.

The Journey to Madinah

For several years, the Prophet Muhammad lived in Makkah. Here, he taught about Allah. Many people listened to Muhammad and became Muslims, like him.

But some people in Makkah did not like Muhammad. They plotted to break into Muhammad's house at night and murder him.

When Muhammad found out about the plot, he asked his cousin Ali to sleep in his house instead of him. Muhammad promised that Ali would not come to any harm.

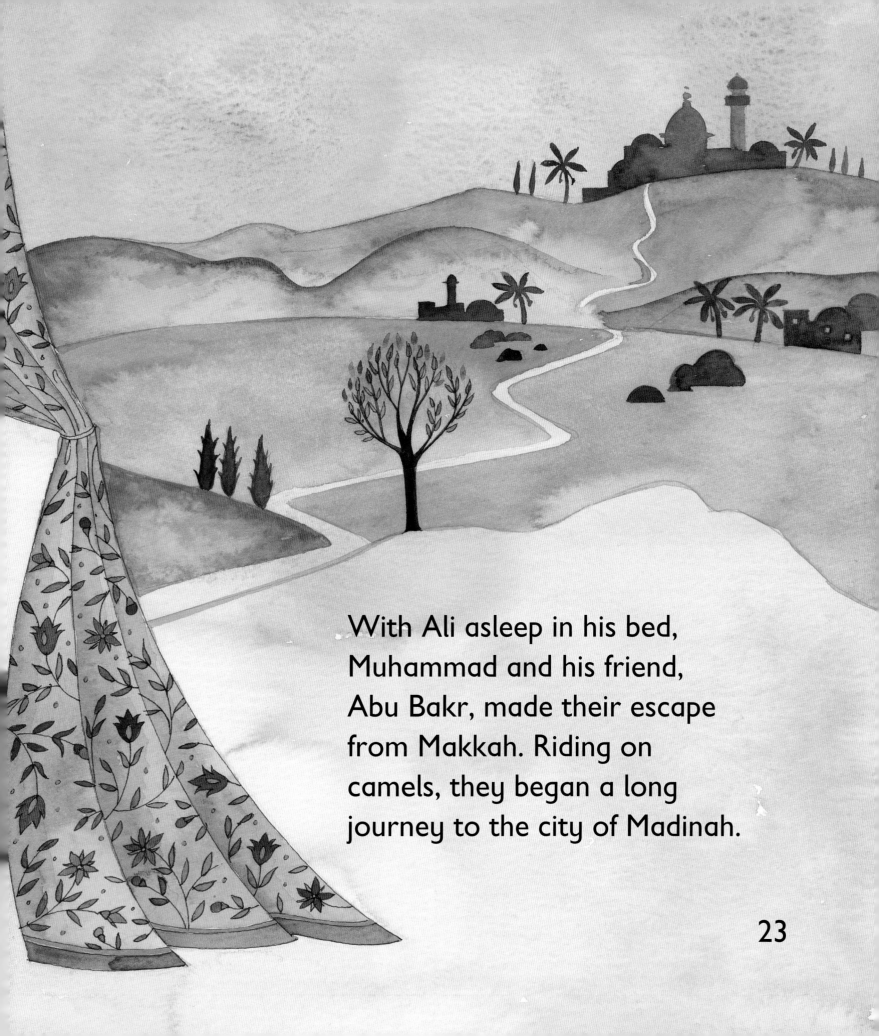

With Ali asleep in his bed,
Muhammad and his friend,
Abu Bakr, made their escape
from Makkah. Riding on
camels, they began a long
journey to the city of Madinah.

23

But, when their enemies came for Muhammad and found Ali in his house instead, they chased after the two friends. Muhammad and Abu Bakr hid in a cave. They knew that Allah would protect them.

And, that is just what happened. A spider spun a huge web all the way across the entrance to the cave. When Muhammad's enemies passed by, they did not stop to look inside the cave.

Muhammad and Abu Bakr were safe in the cave. Allah had protected them, just as they knew Allah would. A few days later, they left the cave and rode off across the desert to Madinah.

It was a long and dusty journey in the baking heat. But, at last, Muhammad and Abu Bakr reached Madinah. There, they were given a warm welcome.

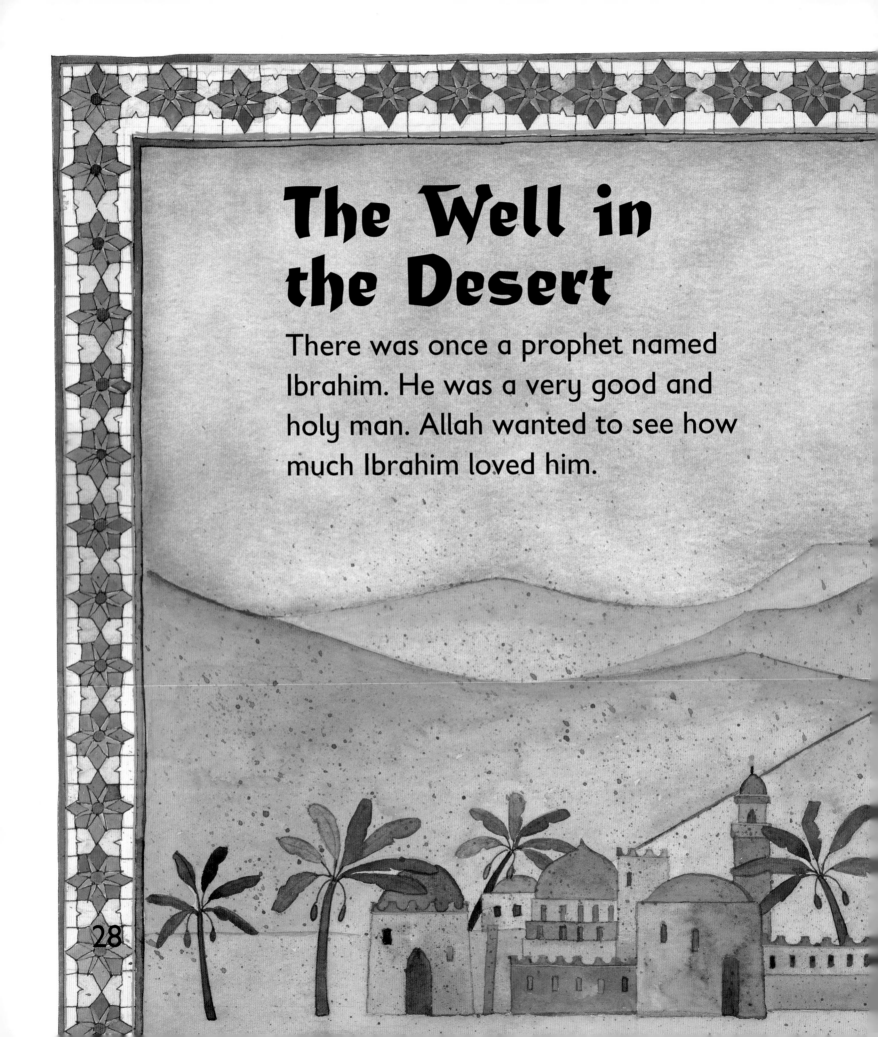

The Well in the Desert

There was once a prophet named Ibrahim. He was a very good and holy man. Allah wanted to see how much Ibrahim loved him.

Allah told Ibrahim to take his wife,
Hajra, and his baby son, Isma'il, into
the desert and leave them there.

29

Ibrahim loved his wife and son
very much, but he was always
ready to do what Allah asked.
So, he took Hajra and Isma'il
into the desert and left
them there all alone.

It was baking hot in the desert. Hajra and Isma'il soon felt very thirsty. But where could Hajra find some water for them to drink?

All around, the desert was dry and dusty. Hajra ran backward and forward between the hills. But she could not find water anywhere.

Suddenly, Hajra heard a voice.
She saw an angel standing next to
her. The angel pointed to where
Isma'il was sitting on the ground.

Hajra looked and saw
water gushing up all
around Isma'il's feet.
She was very happy.
Now there was plenty of
water for them to drink.

34

Hajra said thank you to Allah. She knew that it was Allah who had helped them. He had sent them water when they needed it most.

Notes for Parents and Teachers

About Islam

In Arabic, the word "Islam" means "peace through willing submission to Allah." Muslims (followers of Islam) find peace in submission to the will of God. Allah is the Arabic word for God. Muslims follow Allah's guidance in every aspect of their lives, and believe that Allah is the one true God who created the world and everything in it. They believe that Allah sent messengers, called prophets, to teach people about Islam. Islam was "completed" by the last and greatest prophet, the Prophet Muhammad, who lived in Arabia (modern-day Saudi Arabia) about 1,400 years ago. Muslims believe he received many messages from Allah, which were later collected as the Koran, the Muslims' holy book. To show respect, Muslims often write the letters SAWS after Muhammad's name. These stand for "Sallallahu alaihi wasallam," which means "Peace and blessings of Allah be upon him."

About the stories in this book

In each of the world's religions, stories play an essential part. For centuries, they have been used to teach people about their religious tradition in an accessible way, making difficult ideas and concepts easier to understand. For children in today's multicultural society, these stories also provide an ideal introduction to the different faiths, their key figures, and beliefs.

Muhammad and the Holy Book

This story tells of the first revelation of the Koran to the Prophet Muhammad. Muslims believe that the words of the Koran were revealed by Allah through the angel Jibrail, and therefore, treat the Holy Koran with great respect. They use it as a source of guidance and teaching in every aspect of their lives. The Koran is written in Arabic. Reading, reciting, and studying the Koran is an important duty for all Muslims. The night of the first revelation is remembered by Muslims as Laylat-ul-Qadr (the Night of Power). Muslims try to spend the night in the mosque, praying and reading the Koran.

The Great Night Journey

This journey is an important event for Muslims because, during this time, the command to pray was given by Allah. Prayer is one of the Five Pillars of Islam, five duties that help Muslims to put their beliefs into practice. Allah instructed Muslims to pray five times a day—these daily prayers are called "Salah." By saying their prayers, Muslims believe that they are communicating with Allah. As they say the words of the prayers, they perform a series of set movements. Each set is called a "rak'ah."

The Journey to Madinah

Muhammad's journey from Makkah to Madinah is known as the "hijrah" or "emigration," and took place in the year 622 C.E. This date marks the start of the Islamic calendar. The letters "A.H.," which are written after Muslim years, stand for "the year of the hijrah." The importance of the hijrah lies in Muhammad leaving Makkah, the city of his birth, to become the religious leader of the first Muslim community in Madinah. According to Islamic accounts, the journey took 10–14 days. Muhammad died in Madinah in 632 C.E.

The Well in the Desert

The theme of this story is Allah's testing of the Prophet Ibrahim's love and faith in him. The story is remembered by pilgrims on the Hajj, an annual pilgrimage to Makkah. This pilgrimage is one of the Five Pillars of Islam. All Muslims try to make the Hajj at least once in their lifetime. On their arrival in Makkah, pilgrims walk seven times around the Ka'bah, the most important building in Islam. Then they walk or run between the two nearby hills and visit the well of Zam Zam to remember Hajra's plight. Several other holy sites are also visited on the route before the pilgrims return to Makkah.

Further things to do

• Read the stories aloud to the children and then talk about the stories with them. Ask the children questions about what they think the stories mean. For example, how did receiving the Koran change Muhammad's life?
• Relate the stories to experiences in the children's own lives. For example, have they ever been asked to do something and been afraid of doing it? Do they have books that are special to them, as the Koran is special to Muslims? Have they ever been on a special journey that made them feel happy, as Muslims feel when they are on the Hajj?
• Talk about the life of Muhammad. What special qualities did he have? Talk about role models and people who are significant in the children's lives. Muslims regard Muhammad as a model for living and try to follow his example in their own lives.